Joe Millar

One Night · Two Moons

Paintings by Joe Miller

Published by Joe Miller
374 Industrial Park Drive
Boone, NC 28607

Text copyright © 2013 by Joe Miller
Paintings copyright © 2013 by Joe Miller

Library of Congress Cataloging in Publication Data
Library of Congress Control Number: 2013912382
Miller, Joe. One Night, Two Moons.

Printed by Guangzhou Yi Cai Printing Co. LTD, Guangzhou City, China
8-5-2013
Printed in China

Summary: The Frasier Fir trees on Farmer Brown's Christmas tree farm tire of having to stay in one place. So on the rare occurrence of 2 moons in one night magic transforms the trees into whimsical characters that are now capable of playing musical instruments, dancing and even speaking.
ISBN 9781890052003

I dedicate my book, *One Night, Two Moons* to Emma and Haden Miller, Ashley and Josie Sutton, Meghann Miller, Bailey Ann, Abby and Cade Keller, Macie and Wyatt Keller and Ava Huntley. All who call me Joepops, a sound I love hearing!

Thanks to Sharon Sharpe, my editor, for her help in bringing this book to fruition.

A special thanks to my wife, Lynda, for her constant help and encouragement.

It was a cold and snowy day, and Nana had all of her grandchildren at her house. She was knitting a sweater, and they were getting restless and bored.

"Nana, tell us a story, a new one, please!" said the oldest child. "Yes, Nana, please!" chimed in all the other children.

"Well, let me see . . . how about one from when I was a little girl about your age?" said Nana. "It's about a very magical night on my grandparents' tree farm—something I've never told anyone before."

"Yea! Yea!" they shouted, their eyes growing wide.

So she began . . .

Back in those days, my grandparents, Paw Paw and Maw Maw Brown, lived on a big farm up in the mountains. They had a couple of cows, a big horse, and a few sheep. But mostly, they had Christmas trees, lots and lots of Christmas trees that they grew to sell during the holidays.

Since it takes many years for a tiny seed to grow into a Christmas tree, Paw Paw had to plan ahead. In the springtime he planted tree seeds in what he called "beds." I thought that was funny because there wasn't any mattress, pillow, or blankets—just dirt where the seeds grew! But just like little babies, those seeds stayed right there in their beds and kept growing until they were large enough to be moved to the field with the larger, older trees.

We all watched as Paw Paw hitched Old Buck, his horse, to his wooden sled. Old Buck pulled the children on a sled through Paw Paw's Christmas trees as they searched for the perfect tree. When they finally chose one, Uncle Joseph who had come to help, cut the tree for those boys, and put it on the sled with them.

The boys told Uncle Joseph that they thought it was the most beautiful tree in the world. When Paw Paw overheard them, he felt really good because he took a lot of pride in his trees. I knew that Paw Paw even talked to his trees. He told them it was their job to bring happiness and joy to whoever chose them to take home. "Paw Paw's trees must be very happy!" I thought.

When the sled was full, Old Buck pulled the tree and the children back to their car. It was such fun watching him! He was so big and strong—the biggest horse I'd ever seen. But he was so gentle, and he had the kindest eyes. I loved Old Buck. I think Buck liked me, too.

Some people came from places close to Maw Maw and Paw Paw's farm, and others came from places far away to buy their Christmas trees. Throughout the day they drove down the snowy road, up the snowy road, around the snowy curves by the fence, and through the rows of beautiful trees. Every family was looking for the perfect tree for their home.

One of Paw Paw's friends, Doc Stacy, had a big red tractor he called Chug-Chug. When I heard a certain "a-chug, a-chug, a-chug" sound, I knew that Doc Stacy was on his way to Paw Paw's.

Once there, his grandchildren took off running through the rows of trees, dashing between them, yelling, "Merry Christmas, Trees!" They were having so much fun! I asked Paw Paw if I could run with them. "Sure," he said.

When I caught up to them, one of them asked if I was there to buy a Christmas tree. "No, this is my Maw Maw and Paw Paw's tree farm," I explained.

"Boy, you're lucky!" another one said. "You can have lots of Christmas trees in your house!"

"No," I said, "we just have one, like other people do."

Paw Paw helped Doc Stacy load his wagon with the trees they'd chosen. The kids piled in, and they headed home. Paw Paw and I laughed, listening to "a-chug, a-chug, a-chug" until we could hear it no longer and we knew they had made it back home.

One of Paw Paw and Maw Maw's neighbors, Mr. Adams, brought his big green truck to get trees. He and Paw Paw searched through the rows of trees and picked out the ones he liked. Then, Mr. Adams helped Paw Paw cut them down and load them on his truck.

"Why is Mr. Adams taking so many trees?" I asked.

Paw Paw said, "He takes them to his Christmas tree lot in town to sell to folks who can't get out to the farm." I could tell that Paw Paw was happy that his friend liked sharing the beautiful trees with more people.

Down by Paw Paw's pond two boys about my age were throwing snowballs into the water to watch them make circles. I wanted to throw snowballs, too, but I knew Paw Paw needed my help. Those boys kept throwing one snowball after another! Their dad drove by with a tree tied to the top of the car. He stopped, rolled down the window, and called out, "Come on, boys, it's getting dark!"

As the night drew closer, Paw Paw finished his work. Then we hurried home so we could eat the supper Maw Maw had ready. We were so hungry, we gobbled down fried chicken and beans and mashed potatoes with gravy.

"That was the best supper ever!" I told her.

"Oh, it's just 'cause your Paw Paw worked you so hard!" she replied. "Hurry up, now," she added. "We don't want to be late for the children's program at the church."

Before long we were joining lots of neighbors at the church for the special children's Christmas program. I was excited about seeing some of the friends I hadn't seen in a while! Cade said the opening prayer, Abby quoted Luke's Christmas story, and Bailey sang with Emma and Macie. Wyatt and Haden whispered about some football game. Sisters Meghann and Ashley, who were directing the children's program, looked at them and said quietly, "Not in church, boys." Little Josie and Ava, the youngest of all, slept soundly through the whole program.

Afterward, Paw Paw and Maw Maw and I headed home. There was a feeling of peace and joy in the air. We knew that people were back in their homes, decorating trees, baking cookies, and wrapping gifts. Snow was softly floating to the ground. It was so quiet you could hear a very faint crunch sound as flakes hit the earth. That feeling all around us was what Maw Maw called "Christmas Magic."

Every single person who'd come to Paw Paw and Maw Maw's farm that day had left with a big smile and lots of waves. That made me know they'd gotten more than a beautiful Christmas tree. They'd left with some of the same magic I'd found there!

As we headed back home and passed by lots of trees, I thought I heard a rustling, shaking kind of noise. "Paw Paw," I said, "do you hear that?"

"Hear what?" he replied.

"That noise—it's right here in the trees. Can't you hear it?" I said.

Paw Paw said, "It must be your imagination, since there isn't any wind tonight." I just knew it was the trees, though.

When we got to the house, we settled in by the fire. I was so tired and sleepy I couldn't keep my eyes open. I soon fell asleep in Paw Paw's lap. He carried me into the room where I slept whenever I got to stay overnight, the one I called "my room." It was very warm and cozy with a soft goose-down feather bed and pillow. It was pure heaven sleeping in that bed.

I don't know how long I'd slept, but I was awakened by sounds of crunching snow, laughter, and music. I jumped out of bed and ran to look out the window. When I opened it, I could hardly believe what I saw and heard! There in Paw Paw's tree field were trees running—yes, running with glee!

They were dressed in the most festive elf and Santa-like clothes—outfits with bright reds and greens with white fur trim. They wore stockings of yellow, red, and white, with other colors, too. Some of them were dressed like regular boys and girls. Others were dressed like musicians, and they had musical instruments and were playing beautiful songs I'd never heard before. Others were dancing, shopping, and fishing—doing things I never imagined trees could do.

It wasn't dark, even though it was night. Everything seemed to be glowing! I slipped out the window as quietly as I could, and I began to follow along behind the trees so they couldn't hear or see me. "Where did they get their clothes and shoes from?" I wondered. "What are they doing?"

I had so many questions that I just couldn't stand it any longer. I ran up to a little tree dressed like a girl. Trembling and scared, I finally got up the courage to ask her name. To my joy and amazement, she said, "I'm TreeAnna."

"What a beautiful name," I said. "TreeAnna, can you please tell me what's happening tonight?"

"Well," she replied, "we are all Christmas trees, and our whole lives we have dreamed of making others happy, especially little children. But we are stuck on our stumps. Today was so special for all the people who came to Paw Paw Brown's tree farm that we all thought we would have a little fun ourselves tonight. When everyone was sound asleep, we gathered to have a dance. You will be the only person in the whole world who knows of this, and you must not tell anyone."

"Where did you get your legs? What about your clothes and your shoes and socks?" I said.

"They all appeared like magic," she replied. "Christmas has lots of magic in it, you know."

As I looked around, there were so many magic trees all decked out in their festive clothes. Mr. and Mrs. Bluegreen Tree looked like Mr. Grant Woods' painting "*American Gothic*". Maybe Mr. Woods had seen them before he painted it.

Mr. Fishing Tree was showing off the big fish he'd caught in the pond. Even the fish was decorated for Christmas!

Across the way, I saw Artist Tree doing a wonderful figure painting of one of her tree friends. Maybe she thought she was Georgia O'Keefe.

TreeAnna was there dancing along with her friend SheTree. They stayed close together. I think they were very good friends.

Skinny Tree was with Wide Tree, and they made me think of that nursery rhyme about Jack Sprat and his wife. Momma Shopping Tree was on a spending spree with her friend SpendATree. I wondered what they would buy.

Blueboy Tree thought he should win "Best Dressed." He really was sharp in his colorful outfit!
Dangle Tree had Christmas decorations that jangled as he danced. Kicking Tree tried his best to keep rhythm with the music.

"TreeAnna, it's so light, almost like day!" I exclaimed.

"Yes," she said. "Just look up and you will see why."

There in the sky were two full moons. Never before on one night had I ever seen two moons in the sky at one time. "How can that be?" I asked TreeAnna.

"That's more of the Christmas magic," she said. "Just like the music."

"Yes, it's all magic!" she said.

"Aren't you afraid that all the music and noise will wake up the folks who live around here?" I asked.

"No," she explained. "Only trees and animals can hear and see what we are doing. But tonight, we have given you our special magic so you can see and hear us, too!"

Just before daylight, though, everything began to change. The older trees said their good-byes and began their journey home, back to their stumps. I sensed a fear among the trees. The lighter the sky got, the more excited the trees became. They were removing their clothes and throwing them on the ground. Musical instruments were falling onto the snowy ground as the trees all began to run.

"Look, quick!" I said to TreeAnna. "The trees are running away!"

"No," she said, "they are running back to their stumps. The sun is going to light up the day and warm the air. My family of trees must return to where they grow before that happens. Otherwise, we couldn't live until next Christmas, and that would be very sad. We live so that we can bring happiness to everyone at Christmas, especially to those that believe in magic."

"You must also hurry back to your stump, TreeAnna!" I told her. I really didn't want her to go or see this night end, but I wanted, more than anything, for TreeAnna and all of her friends to be safe. "Hurry, run as fast as you can!" I began to yell at the trees.

The trees scrambled to reach their stumps before it was too late. I could see Paw Paw coming to feed the chickens and sheep, the cows, and of course, Old Buck.

"I hope he doesn't see us!" TreeAnna said. And she took off running as fast as she could. "Good-bye! Merry Christmas!" she called back to me.

I didn't know what to do, so I just called out, "Merry Christmas to you! I'll miss you!"

"You'll see me again someday!" she answered. And then she was gone.

As the sun finally rose above the mountaintop, I stood there and watched the last of the trees settle back on their stumps. Their clothing and musical instruments had already melted in the snow, just like the magic they'd come from. Before Paw Paw could see or hear a thing, every single tree had gotten back home.

No one would ever know about that wonderful night, except me! And I wouldn't tell anyone, because I had made a promise to TreeAnna, my new tree friend.

"Is it okay that you told us, Nana?" asked one of the children.

"Yes," said Nana. "The other night while I was asleep, TreeAnna came to me in my dreams. She looked exactly as she did those many years ago, on that magical night I'd met her on Paw Paw Brown's Christmas tree farm!

"I was startled at first, but she said, 'Don't be afraid. It's me, your friend TreeAnna. I've come to tell you that if you wish, you may tell others what happened that one night with two moons—that night filled with Christmas magic, the night the trees danced about and played music. All of the trees you saw on that night have now found homes as Christmas trees, and it's safe for you to tell our story.' I wanted to talk to her and tell her that I had missed her so much, but I woke up and she was gone.

"After all these years, I have longed to share that wonderful night with others. Now I've told you, since you're so special to me. But wait, there is one more thing."

Nana looked around at each child, one by one. Then she said, "You must watch the night sky closely, and if you ever see two full moons and you hear beautiful music, you will know the Christmas trees are dancing somewhere! And my friend TreeAnna, who never grows old, may just be right there dancing among them!"

HAPPY MAGICAL ENDING, EVERYONE